T0146604

HEAR ME

HEAR ME

BREATHE HOPE

HEAR ME

iUniverse books may be ordered through booksellers or by contacting:

iUniverse
1663 Liberty Drive
Bloomington, IN 47403
www.iuniverse.com
1-800-Authors (1-800-288-4677)

ISBN: 978-1-5320-3519-7 (sc)
ISBN: 978-1-5320-3518-0 (e)

Print information available on the last page.

Library of Congress Control Number: 2017915945

iUniverse rev. date: 10/24/2017

Introduction

> For our struggle is not against flesh and blood, but against the rulers, against the authorities, against the powers of this dark world and against the spiritual forces of evil in the heavenly realms.
>
> —Ephesians 6:12

We should choose to realize that, by exposing the demons that follow us around like hungry cats, pressuring for any amount of food, we are unlocking a truth. Funny as it may sound, but the harder it is on your ego—which is the root of Satan—the more fulfilling it is in the kingdom of God. You can save other souls just by unveiling the truth that is behind the half-awake masks we choose to wear daily. As a result of the pain and/or suffering that every one of us feels daily on any type of scale, we have the power with Christ Jesus to use what we are trying to fight by ourselves and grab a hold of his perfect peace, the Lord's knowing, the Father's almighty ways.

The root of the truth is that if you allow Jesus to protect, guide, and help you, he will. I challenge everyone to expose a demon that won't seem to get off their backs. Call that draining spirit out! Tell us all about him or her, and expose every detail. The honesty is that if you can see in all of your heart to trust God in what you are about to expose to the world, it will hit that one person who needed to know he or she is not alone! We all will have our Judases who are out to try to hurt and betray us. But our lives are about the truth and pulling others out of an endless hole that seems impossible to get out of. With the truth (Jesus), we can comfort, uplift, motivate, and truly feel each other's souls.

I will tell you all, with all the love in my heart, I struggled for years with a drug problem as well as many other things. I depended on different types of drugs to help me escape my present reality, to keep running from my past, and to drown out any possibility of a defeating future. That spirit of escape ate my soul. I have forgotten a lot of my life due to the invite I gave to all sorts of these different effect-giving demons. I lived with mind-eating guilt, blood-drinking shame, and a hate for myself that could wipe out the ocean.

Now I have no guilt and shame, and I am forgiven for all the actions that came along with finding my fixes. All the glory and peace goes to Jesus. He saved me from death multiple times. I have hit rock bottom. I have experienced part of hell on earth that I would not wish upon my worst enemy. Please, whoever is reading this, know that this is just one of many revelations of the group of flesh eaters that were my spiritual posse for so long. Please know that, whatever you have experienced or are currently fighting, I truly with honest love understand you! I want to tell you that, with the love that Jesus washed me with, I love you. I know what it is like to feel like you are locked in a cage in your mind, body, or soul, but I am here to also tell you, "There is always a road out, no matter what your past or present time looks like." The directions to this road are repentance and faith. Jesus is waiting. I promise, he was waiting there for me.

I sit here in my spirit, looking at the door that leads to my past. I am standing here, looking at a ten-foot giant made out of black, solid, shiny wood. The door has a presence about it that makes one want to run away and sprint until the door is no longer in existence. I have realized that, the harder I ran, the harder I would stumble. I would stumble right back at the foot of this terrorizing door.

There is no running. I am shaping countless circles of my past into my present by trying to flee. This door has no appealing desire. I stand here looking at the shadows of the past and decide I would take myself out of the knowing that this darkness is mine to be opened. I decide that this door would be opened now in a different light. I am going to be an observer of my past and not a victim. I will not be effected to what I will see once I walk through the door. The light in my spirit suddenly changes to a beautiful light yellow color surrounding the door. There is no fear in entering back any longer. My heart is set on observing the ever so weighty memories so I may give my experience to someone else in hopes he or she may change the way he or she looks at his or her door of the past.

1

Initial Implant

We all have a first memory. I pray that yours is of peace
and love. Mine, however, crept into my heart, mind, and
spirit at a different angle. This memory shoots to my heart
at the speed of anger and the angle of misunderstanding,
and the conclusion is set at hurt. My first emotional wall
was built at the age of two years old. I am standing here
in my spirit, looking in as a third party.

I see myself as a little girl with hardly any hair. I am
innocent in all areas of my being. I am happy in my little
spirit. I am in love with the fact that I am hanging out
with my daddy. I see myself standing on the right side of
my dad, pulling on his pants leg, barely being able to talk.
Both he and I are standing in front of a bookshelf with
lots of items, one specifically being a football.

To me, at two years old, the bookshelf looks like a
skyscraper. I am mumbling, trying to talk, and telling
him I want the football. I am pointing right at it and
whining because he wouldn't get it down for me. He is

just staring at me with a blank, vacant face. I am confused as to why he wouldn't help me.

In my spirit, I know I have played with that ball before. The ball is a familiar friend to me, but my father's reaction is not. All of a sudden, I see in my spirit the demon of anger enter into my father. He loses his mind. He starts screaming in rage so loud that I immediately start crying, and I feel my little spirit leave my body and run away in fear. I shut down. My body is an emotional wreck. I feel sick to my stomach. I couldn't understand why he is yelling at me. To me, it is not what he is saying that affects me.

Obviously at two years old, words are not what I lived knowing, but feeling and sight is my two-year-old mind's way of processing a situation. The negativity and evil that my father has exposed me to at that moment result in loss of a piece of my innocence, trust, and freedom. The first brick is laid in building my house of protection around my soul. At two years old, I would learn how to disassociate myself from my current situation, therefore resulting in the initial implant of trauma.

2

Hear Me

Honestly as I begin to move in my spirit, going to the next available memory, there is a huge time lapse. In my spirit, I am walking through a tunnel of static. I am waiting for this box to come shooting at me through the tunnel walls like a messenger dropping off mail. I am waiting and waiting, but the static goes on and on. Then finally out comes a box from the side of my unconscious tunnel. Another memory is ready for me to open. I jump right in.

I see that I am about five years old. I am screaming so loud that the tears would not stop running down my face. I am kicking and punching the hardwood floor. I get up and move my dresser drawer in front of my door so no one could get into my room. I fall back down to the floor, screaming so hard and loud that all the blood rushes to my head. My eyes feel like they are going to explode out of my head.

Interestingly I do not remember anything before or after this aggressive tantrum. According to some, I did this often enough for them to think Satan spiritually possessed me. I have my understandings of why I acted the way I did. Satan did not possess me. I was left to defend myself in the physical world against a demon larger than I was.

Putting my spirit back into the mind-set I was in at five years old, I can tell you I am screaming in pain. I want someone to save me; I need someone to hear me. But what am I screaming about? That answer, I believe, comes along in later memories. It looks like I have mastered the craft of disassociation at the small age of five.

The urgency of this memory lies in the feelings that are running through my veins. These feelings are like unwanted drugs that are taking over and overcoming my entire being. I am scared, lonely, misunderstood, and angry. I feel like I need to run away, and the strongest feeling of them all would be loss. I feel like I am trapped and have no way out of my body at that moment. I am stuck. Something happened prior to the episode of rage that made my spirit and mind trapped in my body, unable to check out and leave.

This is where I first encounter my personal demon. He has made a home inside me. He fills the hole, the feeling of loss in this memory, with himself. He buries deep in my heart like a hungry tick on a deer. He fills me with his tornado of destruction.

At five years old, I meet rage. He shows me a form of expression I never knew existed within me. At that moment, I hate a piece of myself.

3

BLACK CAT

In this continuing journey, I realize I have no time to sit in my tunnel of static. There's no time to let the section of my mind become anxious with wondering which memory would decide to expose itself next. I am immediately standing dead center of what I call my personal mousetrap. I see myself laying lifeless on the trap. The metal has snapped shut right on my heart, keeping me stuck here for years to follow. I look to my left and immediately realize the solidity of this memory. Why is this so solid? Everything in this memory is touchable. It's like someone asking you to picture a black cat in your mind. You see the cat. He is touchable, knowable, and real to all of your physical and spiritual senses. This is my black cat.

I am trying to get into this memory for you, but it is not easy or favorable for my physical body and mind to even want to open my spiritual eyes and look at what I see. My physical body right now at this moment is starting to manifest feelings within itself. At this present time, as I stand between both worlds, my spirit is pulling me with confidence and strength into this war zone, but my body is screaming, "Not again!" I have realized that this "not again" feeling has kept me stagnant for so long. In turn, there is no progress in healing or letting go. In knowing this, I will continue.

At this moment in my physical body, my throat hurts. I feel as if there is a rope around my neck, and it is just getting tighter and tighter. My heart is pounding so fast and hard that I can hear it screaming at me, telling me to "Stop moving forward!" My stomach feels like it is being turned like clothes tossing wildly in a dryer. The heaviest physical pain I feel is my chest. My chest feels like it is being compressed between two rocky boulders. It feels like it's crushing into pieces, making it almost impossible to breathe. While all this is taking place in my physical body, I try to stay focused on the outcome of looking my black cat directly in the eyes.

Now I find myself in my spirit at twenty-seven years old, looking at my approximately five- to six-year-old naked self sitting in a bathtub. I am sitting toward the back of the tub. The water is running. My six-year-old self looks lifeless, frozen, paralyzed in the spirit. I see a man get in the tub with me.

All of a sudden now, my twenty-seven-year-old spirit has placed itself in my five- to six-year-old body during the remainder of this memory. I believe this is taking place so I may explain better the feelings I did not understand how to handle at such a young age.

I am face-to-face with a grown man. We are sitting in the bathtub together. This would be the first time I would see a man's penis. This man has decided he would gift me with this experience. I can tell you that it is not a gift I would want anyone to be forced to have presented to him or her in such a manner as this. I know something is not right. I know I am face-to-face with a demon. I know I am too little to run or escape. I have no way out of the tub. This is where I would encounter my first gut feeling of what is wrong, evil, not of God.

The feeling of the difference between right and wrong is branded into my soul so deep that there would never be a gray line in myself again. Everything is good or bad, right or wrong, black and white from that moment on. The experience taking place in the tub at that moment shapes the core of my belief, being, ways, knowledge, and feelings toward myself and others. At that moment, the rest of the brick is quickly laid to finish the house of protection around my soul. I lock the doors tight. But somehow the demon I meet that day makes a large room for himself inside my house.

Corruption ensures he makes himself comfortable.

4

GOLDEN TICKET

I have the understanding with myself that I could go into every single memory and try to figure out the whys, but for the safety of my mind, I choose not to. I can tell you from experience that it is not about all the mess and dusty detail of what happened and how. It is about the feelings, emotion, and the implanted pains picked up along the way, going through each experience. So my goal is just to hit the initial implants for the understanding of this journey. With all this being said, my spirit has taken me eight years ahead through my tunnel.

I sit here now looking at my fourteen-year-old self. Once again I choose to reenter my body for a better perspective of what I am going through, feeling, thinking, and doing. I would describe this as healing time travel. At this point in my life, I have just entered freshman year of high school, which is already a growing pain in itself. I am not mentally or emotionally involved in school. I believe that is due to the waterfall of family problems that flood my mind daily. On top of it all, I have what is called a learning disability. I could barely read or write. I trust in my heart that was the result of early childhood trauma. Then again, that's my truth. I am not a doctor.

I sit in my spirit, and I see a large bowl the size of a king-sized bed. In that vessel, I have puberty, family issues, high school drama, struggling schoolwork, and my desire to just find peace, all mixed together to make a roller-coaster, emotion-filled soup. I look up past the large soup bowl and see the memory start to play out. Here we go.

It is my first high school party. I am walking around, making sure everyone is having fun. My stomach is turning in excitement and enjoyment. I feel a sense of relief having all these people at my house, my party. I am so excited that I could provide them all with a place to just relax. I also feel a sense of physical protection and belonging with all my friends around me. I am walking downstairs in my basement, and I run into a guy friend, whom we will call Joe.

Joe proceeds to introduce me to one of his really close friends. This is where I fall into deep passion for the first time with his friend, alcohol. Soon I come to realize, after the first three shots of her, alcohol would be my golden ticket to my false place of peace.

I have been searching for this type of escape from reality for so long, and she warms my body with her delusional comfort and false theories. I surrender immediately to her open, web-tangled arms. I let go of all of my control, and I give it to alcohol. She runs my being. She speaks for me, and she also blacks me out.

After letting alcohol have her ride in my body, she leaves me for dead. She is a vampire demon, but I am addicted to her bite.

I lay helplessly, coming to the true realization that things and people are around me that I don't want to be there. That's funny to me because I felt physically protected at one point earlier in this memory. Oh, how the truth is always revealed. I need help, but no one wants to step in. The friends I thought I felt protected by earlier feed off my weakness at that very moment and use me as their playground. It seems alcohol has control over them, like little puppets on a string. We are all just a part of her twisted, foul game. There is no protection from her wrath. I am in and out of consciousness.

The loss of control over my mind and body is now at a point where my spirit realizes it is playing with death. Fear kicks in, along with misunderstanding, sorrow, and grief. I am pleading with myself in my mind to just throw up to somehow live through this black moment.

Even through all this, I still keep my golden ticket in my right hand and my newfound false friend, alcohol, in my left for many years after that. Despite her vicious ways, she is a crutch to all the things I could not face without her. The moments of escape from reality are worth more to me than my own life. I would play alcohol's tricky games. Every time I did this, the vampire would get stronger by feeding off my spirit. I would be playing with death, digging myself deeper into an unawareness of nothing.

5

SECURITY BLANKET

I fly past memory after memory, seeing them all sown together like a homemade quilt my grandmother would have made for me. Although this quilt feels like a servant of the evil one has specially made it, I see all the same underlying feelings of pain. Then I come to a bone-chilling stop. I feel the presence of a different sort of evil. I haven't run into this feeling in years. The taste of metal and iron fill my mouth. My body is physically reacting to what I am encountering in the spirit. I am twitching, panting like a dog on a hot summer day. My whole body is going numb. I feel like a thousand stones are being placed on my shoulders. The weight of the world has overcome my entire existence.

I quickly look at what I am facing. I see a stairwell that is going down into a pit of thorns the size of elephant tusks. I walk down, only to step in the very middle of the earthquake. I look around helplessly. My scene changes before my eyes. I am fifteen years old, looking at my mature body in the mirror of my bathroom. I am staring myself eye to eye.

I ask my fifteen-year-old self, "What is going on?"

I reply with a bloodcurdling scream that comes from the depth of my being. This shriek says it all. After all these years, I have picked up so much filth and destruction from others that it has become so much of who I am.

My soul needs to be heard. I want to be set free from my racing, poison-filled thoughts that are haunting me day and night, giving me no relief, taking away any understanding of myself I thought I had, owning me. I am being tortured by my past and robbed of the present moment. Anxiety rapes me of my future to come. Everything around me turns black. This would be the darkest form of existence. I am stuck inside my mind, the casing where my soul was planted, much like a flower placed in a soil-filled pot. I am rooted in with all the demons that made themselves at home. I am facing them, but I am not ready to defeat them. I don't know how. I am screaming to escape, but I couldn't leave. Help me. I couldn't cry, move, breathe, or just be. I need to somehow get back to my present moment. I am trapped. I quickly realize that this darkness I am trapped in was, in fact, hell itself.

The voices of each demon are tormenting me. Their voices are like announcers over an intercom, and a personal weapon of destruction fills their hands. Their voices become like nails on a chalkboard, telling me I am worthless, useless, stupid, filthy, and used. They are saying I am nothing and would never be loved. They are asserting I am a monster, just like them.

I feel them closing in like cannibals that haven't eaten in weeks. I have to get out. But how? At that very moment, I form my own weapon against them, my vehicle back to reality, my wooden ladder out of this hell, my way out of the wolves' den the demons formed joyfully for their pleasure. I come back to reality. I can breathe. I can see. The voices of torment are silenced. I look in the mirror to notice blood pouring down my face.

I look in my right hand, and I am holding my weapon tightly. I have used a sharp piece of metal to cut myself from the corner of my eye to the edge of my mouth. Feeling my face pulsing with physical pain lets me know I am still alive. I experience at that moment that I have some sort of control over the things that haunt me daily. I finally learn to shut them up, to harness them like wild bulls. The redness of the blood keeps me knowing that a piece of me is still aware.

The marking would form a scar on my face and stay for years to follow. I brand myself. No one wants to hear my voice, so I let the scars speak for themselves. My new weapon gives me temporary strength. My personal physical affliction would be the portal back to the moment of now. My security blanket is formed. I take it with me everywhere.

6

SATAN'S CHILD

All I have been is honest with you about my thoughts, ways, and moments of the past. I need to confess that, as I go deeper and come closer to my present-time memories, it is getting harder for me to want to write, to even find the words to start processing the next mindless adventure I created for myself. I feel that, as I get to the neighboring memories of my present moment, I am dragging a spirit of depression around with me. I believe this feeling is lingering so closely because I am just fresh out of the cycle of these next handful of incidents.

There is also the understanding with myself that I am of adult age in these memories, and despite the foundation of my past, I have my free will. I know the difference between right and wrong, the road to hell and the route to heaven.

Throughout the next part of my life, I seem to have always been feeding, depending, and camping on the road to hell. I feel like I am stepping on my own eggshells. I am afraid of myself at this moment. I fear to make myself angry, sad, or depressed. I am frightened that I will hate myself again. I don't want to ever feel like I did before. I am stopping now to say a prayer.

> I pray, Lord, that you hear my cry. I pray, Father, that you send your war angel down from heaven to keep my mind, body, and spirit protected from any evil that will try to attack me emotionally during this next memory. Lord, push me through so others will understand they are not alone in this evil, desire-filled world. Help me to expose these demons that lurk around, hunting us down like prey. They will not feed on us any longer. Our chains will be broken in Jesus's name I pray. Amen.

I step out of this world into the portal of my mind. My spiritual eyes are strengthened and opened. I feel my angel standing behind me with the power of God and the strength of honest love. All events start to play out.

I've just had my first child at twenty years old. There's no family to support or help me. My daughter's father would be facing fifteen years to life for selling drugs to an undercover police officer in a school zone. He is arrested immediately. I have no idea what is going on until the officers show up at my front door with guns in my face to ask me questions. Neither my daughter's father nor I ever touched a drug. He has fallen into this money game with a gang, trying to make a quick ten thousand dollars to pay the bills and house mortgage. His job is not providing the funds he needs. We are stuck in this world, the pressure of money problems, statutes, and wants. The life we are supposed to provide for our child takes over his being and sends him to the cages of the earth, prison.

He has snapped under pressure. I soon would take that plunge into the cages of this world. My enclosure would be set for me on the streets. I depend morning, noon, and night on my truly close but painful friend, alcohol. I rely on the escape from myself. I need to feel like I am living in a fairy tale. I build my world around the foundation of corruption. All I care about is me. But all I hate is me. How can you care and hate at the same time? I am self-righteously looking for the next rush, thrill, escape, and dance with death. In turn, I am hurting others.

In the times I would come down from a three- to seven-day party binge, the demons I danced with for seven days are angry I stopped playing with them so they would talk me down to nothing until I pick up alcohol and start once again. I think I am taking myself through the foggy, distorted cycle of healing. Soon I would get really tired of alcohol's same furious cycle. It starts to feel like chewing a piece of stale gum for eternity.

I am nothing short of over it. I need something more. I feel the filth just burning within me. Every demon I have met since birth has made a personality of its own inside my mind. They would fight over how to destroy me. Soon they all would be giggling like little children watching a clown perform. They would all meet their silencer of pleasure, and I would encounter the devil himself, disguised as an angel of light.

He has shown up like Prince Charming coming to rescue me from my pit of hate, but only to bring me to the land of self-loathing and destruction. He presents me with a box. I open the box to find a small, powdery, white mountain.

Cocaine takes me right into her slop, like a skier on a black diamond. At that moment, I marry my life with cocaine. I feel like I couldn't see, think, be, or live without her. I feel as if I were given some sort of supernatural power over everything I knew. I have control over all situations and people until she rips my mind into tiny shreds as she slowly fades away and I come crashing down. I need more of her! Always! She can never fade away again. I know, if cocaine's rush, strength, and power left me, my mind would shut down, and it would turn fatal. Being a woman, I receive a lot of my addiction for free, but when I don't, the need for cocaine's world takes my spirit and flesh through all accounts to get back into my newfound fairy tale.

She disguises herself so well. Her false since of control blends in my path of life so perfectly, like a thick, sharp bear trap covered with beautiful leaves. I keep dodging the death grip of the trap until I walk right into the snap. I would find myself in the hospital overdosing. My superpowers are gone. My world turns to blood, and all I feel is my chest wanting to explode. It feels like an animal is trying to escape my body. I am dying.

My mistake is thinking I have control over the sinful

power of the drug. Truth is, the drug always had me. I decide to deny at those moments in my existence that I am submitting myself to addiction. Cocaine tries to prove the boasting of its healing cure on my mind. There is no cure. It only adds gasoline to the already blazing forest fire. And now it wants to prove it could take me out of this world. I come out of my own personally mocked up crime scene alive and breathing. I look at myself in the mirror, and I have lost everything—my daughter and any form of control. Any piece of self-worth I was holding onto is burned in her flames.

The things I do to keep this drug by my side are unforgivable. I am staring closely into my soul at twenty-one years old, and at that moment, I see hell screaming with pleasure. Another one of Satan's children is born.

7

Trust in Man

Repeating the same self-righteous routines day after day, seeking the next thrill in Satan's playground (this world), take me straight to the fun house of my mind. I see myself walking through a dark hallway with a hundred sinful doors to choose from. By this time in my life, I have walked through them all. I couldn't recognize myself anymore. I couldn't even see a glimmer of who I truly am. It's like looking in the mirror at a fun house. You are short, and your head is the size of Texas. Your eyes look like black beans, and your hair looks like a bowl full of noodles. You have a knowing that, despite what you are visually seeing, you do not truly look like that. Unfortunately I lose any knowing of myself inside and out. I feel like I am going crazy.

Am I mentally ill? Am I sick? Someone needs to fix me. I seek out doctor after doctor, five different therapists, and anyone who would listen. I would walk in, sit down, and talk to them like they were the support system I never had.

I am twenty-one to twenty-two years old, seeking guidance, love, truth, help, and understanding of myself and the ways of my mind. I come to some very dark dead ends with each person I would encounter. I come to find that the motives behind the listening ears are filled with lust or gossip or interested in trying new medications. I am put on all different kinds of pills. Yes, they tame the voices of the demons, but the medicine never rips out the roots of pain to clear the misunderstanding and guilt that is eating me alive daily. I need someone to help me get to the root of the cause of my chaotic mind, to tell me I am okay, strong, lovable. I want someone to tell me I can be healed. I put all my trust in man, their words, worldly wisdom, truths, experiences, promises, and protection.

I believe in my fellow neighbors who call themselves trustworthy, only to realize I put my soul in the hands of the wrong resources. At that time in my life, I turn cold, closed off, and more self-seeking then I have ever been. I feel like no one on this entire planet understands me. I just need to confess my pain and sin without being judged, ridiculed, or put on anymore medication. But in trying to be set free by man, I am made a case to each one. I am made a problem, a statistic. I am labeled bipolar, amongst all sorts of other things. It's like a cat being born from a horse. I have never been seen or heard of before, and my case is extreme. I believe all of their lies. I put all my trust and heart into the wrong hands.

8

SOMETHING MORE

I sit here now looking at my next memory on the projector screen of my mind. This one is in such close contact that it's as if it's in 3-D. I am twenty-four years old. This memory will only be three years back. I am extremely conscious, aware, and hypersensitive in this memory. It's as if I can sit here and have a mature conversation with myself inside the memory. It feels like there is a film of goop over the entire scene. The goo is making itself known as the dirtiness that laid upon the relationships I fall into during these times.

I see a man. We will call him Sam. Sam, now in this present day, is my ex-husband. We meet, get married, and stay together for a short time. He is involved in Scientology. I stay in Scientology for about a year or more. I believe there is a God. I know of the Bible. But I never truly know or have a relationship with God at this time in my life. There is a yearning in my soul for something more. I have been rotting inside myself for so long that I jump on the opportunity to get involved in Scientology, like an ant on syrup.

My personal truth is that God gave the man who started Scientology a natural healing process, but then he turned everything God revealed to him into a self-fulfilling glory for his own self. He gave nothing back to God. Scientology has the right underlying, basic understanding that trauma and memories that your mind is holding affects your physical body. Negative energy needs to be released. But they leave out God. In my knowing, the last thing you want to do is leave God out of anything. I have no further want or need to speak on the subject of Scientology. It is what it is. We all have moments that we look back on and say to ourselves, "What in the world was that?!"

At this time, Sam and I have moved from Nashville to Birmingham, Alabama, to open up a bar. Yes, my friend alcohol comes in all different shapes, colors, and sizes, and I am in charge of serving her deceitful appeal to all of our customers. I find that I am living in a merry-go-round of existence. I start to see that my life is playing the same horrifying scenarios over and over again.

At twenty-four years old, working at a bar in a world based around one's image, beauty, sex appeal, worldly wisdom, and desires of the flesh, I am drowning in disbelief that this is the rest of my life. My guilt, shame, and distrust in others and myself keep me from having any real, solid relationships. I believe that everyone has his or her own desires and no one is honest in trust, love, and understanding. Maybe it is because I have become a monster of my own and couldn't seem to see any good in myself. In turn, I am seeing evil in everything and everyone around me. I am miserable. I couldn't stand my job.

I see others drowning in their sorrows right along with me. The bar is a cesspool full of masked souls trying to cover up all the sin, truth, and reality that exist in them. Unfortunately alcohol likes to expose the truth in a condescending, backbiting, and angry, predictable manner. I have over a thousand of my dungeon dwellers with me every weekend. I am over it. I am finished with the cycle of lust, greed, and "poor me" attitudes. I stick with my job due to an addiction for quick money and lots of it. I am making enough money to do everything I want to do, go wherever I desire to go, buy anything my flesh desires, or feed whatever addiction burns within me.

But guess what? I still am hurting inside and battling anxiety, stress, anger, headaches, and self-mutilation. And hate just keeps brewing within me about my past. I can tell you firsthand that money fixes nothing. It buys no amount of forgiveness, worth, happiness, or joy. One cannot purchase sanity, peace, or real truth. So here we go, another riddle is solved. Money is not the answer to my problems. I bleed, ache, and search for something more. I need to know the truth to myself. Some relationships come and go.

Sam and I are divorced due to trust issues, non-communication, or matched-up realities. There are a lot of underlying differences that we have, so that relationship is in the air like vapor. And before the gas could disappear, I am pregnant with Bane's child.

Who is Bane? Well, Bane would be a man I have just met. This would be the same cycle of how my daughter came to be. I see it repeating, and I sink in my spirit, only desiring the best for my child to come. I want it to be different this time around—a family and true, honest love. I want Bane to want me, need me, and love me. But we just met at the bar a month before. So what is to come about this mess I have created once again in my world?

The chaos just seems to follow me like a shadow on asphalt. I have taken a pregnancy test to find out that God is giving me a second chance to get right and raise this child. I swear I would not repeat the same dance with all these demons as I willingly did before. I know that all evil wanted to do was rip this opportunity from me. They want my blessing. The ones I trusted tell me to abort my child. It would be better to wait to have a baby. Now is not the right time. I find throughout my life that evil loves to and will speak boldly through others. I feel hell calling through their nail-biting words. But I would not entertain their demands.

At that moment, a piece of my soul comes gasping up out of the filth and scum it was buried under and looks up at the sky. My soul makes a breakthrough from some worldly existence. My soul speaks to heaven for me. At that moment, I am given the grace to feel God. I am lifted out of myself into a reality thicker than this world, much like releasing a butterfly from the palms of your hand. I am no longer stuck in myself. I have space that feels like eternity. There is no evil dwelling in this moment. I feel an overwhelming calming in the pit of my stomach, something unexplainable. There is, in fact, something more.

Then I come crashing back into my body and the depths of sickness in my mind, once again into all the voices that storm me daily. The demons are holding on to me like I am a balloon tied to a string. They are all holding onto this string and wouldn't let me go that easily. Do they understand at that moment a piece of my soul was just brought back to life? I am made a little stronger then I had been before they welcomed me back. I would make that experience of my "something more" a part of my DNA from that moment on. I had been given a divine weapon of truth that was undeniable to my spirit.

9

NOTHING LEFT

I need to express that I usually write every day. This time I have had a gap in my mind filled with no desire at all to confront this next go-around. Why, why, why does it have to be like this? Why do I have to see so much confusion, pain, and hurt? Why do I have to cause so much hurt and so many tornadoes? Why do Bane and I have to live through the outcome of our pasts just for it to leak in and infect our present moments together with disaster?

I am screaming "Why?" in my spirit. Then it hits me like raindrops on a hot blacktop. I start to cool off from my rampage of "whys" filling my mind with dead-end results. The "why mes" get me stuck. Why not me? Why not me? We all go through a variety of experiences with different details attached to them, but there is some sort of rooted, main, underlying cause of my pain. This I know is true to me. Once I recognize the causing root, the irritating splinter, and where it is located, I feel like I can expose the demon and, with the strength of Christ, be loosened from the chains of the incidents.

The "why me" episode stops now. It does not matter why. What is fulfilling and peaceful is understanding that whatever trapped time warp of evil we were in is now over with. It's done. Gone. And in my truth, it will continue to stay away from me. He is all-knowing, and he will protect his children. My Father stands strong in his promises and protection. And with this strength, I will jump on this spiritual ship and sail down through the storm of the past.

Bane and I move in together right away. As soon as I find out I am carrying a child, I quit smoking, drinking, taking drugs, and popping pills like they are Tic-Tacs. The "something more" that I make a part of my DNA that night is Christ. I trust and believe I have activated my faith that evening.

I deny the demon's voice of opinion on aborting my child. I set another soul before mine. I put someone else before me. In that moment, I defeat a piece of self-righteousness, a segment of Satan. The root of Satan is self-righteousness, egocentrism, ego, or anything that has to do with self. His root is exposed and crushed for that moment in time. So my soul is able to speak and pray to heaven that night. I am activated in my faith and, by grace, given the faith to feel the power of his hand and make it known to my spirit. I feel deep down that I want to have a solid family unit. I do everything in my being to get Bane on board.

But things do not go as I imagined in my mind. I have a fairy-tale life mocked up for me and my child to come. I would be married and live in a beautiful, safe neighborhood. My husband and I would be deeply in love with each other. We would have lots of money and an honest, open relationship. I would finally be able to just be me. The list goes on and on about details I have specifically put together in my mind of how my life would be from this moment on. None of the wishes I desire for myself come true during this time in our relationship.

That moment of bliss with God slips right through my fingers. I have no healing process on my past issues, and I know nothing about Bane's history or details of rooted feelings he has carried with him into our relationship. The two of us just come together and act like we both are in perfect peace with ourselves and each other.

I will tell you that demons like to play hide-and-seek, Marco Polo, or tag. Their specialty is to make you feel like you are a swinging piñata, just waiting for the bat to hit your ribs. Bane's demons slowly start to expose themselves. His demons activate my personal demons and trigger memories from my past.

So we can see here that Bane and I have come together as one couple living under the same roof, having a baby, and now sharing bills and knowing nothing about each other. When we do decide to talk and communicate, it is very surface conversation. We are too afraid to share the truth and nothing but the whole truth about ourselves. We are both afraid of judgment from each other.

Bane and I both have a common root of pain linked to judgment that has been cast upon us from ones we trusted emotionally to lean on in our lives. All of the negative spirits that we had attached to us are brought under one household. They have a field day on our minds.

Bane and I start to devour each other spiritually, verbally, physically, and emotionally. I am not big into getting into too much detail of incidents, but I feel like it is of importance to understand the subjects of pain we placed into each other's lives. I feel the placement on each other is due to the brick houses Bane and I spent our whole lives individually building for our own protection. We would not let each other in to help one other. We couldn't even help ourselves. Neither of us trusts anyone or any feeling. Everything in our lives is always a temporary relationship, high, feeling, or emotion. Neither of us knows what it is like to be truly at peace and joyful. We have no sympathy or empathy for one another. Our hearts ultimately deep down inside are good, beautiful, and selfless. Bur our brick houses are built so large that I could not break down his, and he could not take any weapon to mine and knock it down.

So here we are in a physically abusive, sexually perverted relationship, verbally ripping each other apart daily. Bane finds ways of escape and pleasure in other women, and I would be on the constant run back and forth from Nashville to Birmingham. We seek counseling together. We try everything. But our demons over the years learn how to be deceitful and charming and portray a "who me?" attitude. We are living in an UFC fighting ring. Our coaches are rage, anger, and ego. The heat on our arguments and even now daily conversations are as hot as hell itself. We are going to end up killing each other.

The tornado of destruction that would come through

once a month has caused multiple arrests for Bane and constant buildup of residue on our relationship. We are still holding on in the moments of silence between each other to a hope that we could truly see each other's purity and love one another. But things just turn black, especially after our son is born.

My feelings then are, if the spirit of rage causes Bane to accidentally hurt my son, I feel like I would kill him. Our son would end up with one dead parent and another in jail for life. Bane and I just keep walking deeper and deeper into a dark cave. There is no light to guide us through. All the pain we create for each other leaks into the minds and knowledge of our families. Now we have third parties and their opinions involved. Bane and I are being individually fed ideas of doubt and ultimately left misguided and lost.

We need prayer, a miracle, help, peace, and strength. We both want to be healthy mentally for each other and our son. But how? And who will be able to break through our thick skulls and reach our screaming souls? I have nothing left but the shed next to my brick house of protection. My shed would be any hope I had left.

10

IT'S TIME

I have come to many realizations and understandings about myself throughout my life's journey. I believe and trust that, if one takes the time to process one's past in a third-party mind-set, one will see why exactly one faced the incidents one did and how the tiniest detail about oneself is built off all the incidents one encountered. Once I came to actually know myself through Christ, my life became clear. One interesting knowing about myself is that I am very spiritually sensitive. For example, I can only write out doors. It's funny. But if I do not give myself the spiritual space I need, I would be sitting inside, wracking my brain with anxiety and unwanted pressure. In my mind, I feel like a hamster on a stationary wheel. All I can say is "No thanks" without looking too deep into my need for spiritual space. My reason for sharing this small item of truth about myself with my readers is so they may come to realize that their spirit man speaks to them. The Holy Spirit speaks to them.

When our heart truly, deep down inside is pure and of

good, it is in our best interest to become familiar with our spirit man and the connection with the unseen through faith as well as the knowing of truth that is attached within us. Why would I make myself sit inside, causing stress and anxiety, when I know for a fact a way to relieve the anxiety and relax my being is to be outside? I guess one could call this awareness of spiritual and physical health or the Holy Spirit's guidance to healing. I trust that, when we explore positive self-care with the Lord, the peace in the positivity leads to selflessness. So leaning into the healing and awareness of the Holy Spirit will lead to less attention on self. Push back ego and then have the ability to help others because of the personal positive understanding one has with oneself and the journey. You know who you are so there is no spirit of confusion allowed in your equation of life. I feel like, once I knew me, I was able to help pull others out of their darkness. My key, secret, and safe zone is to know Christ Jesus.

This next flash of delight would be the work of the Lord's hand. I come now into this uplifting memory. This would be the start of my cleansing with the Lord. At this time in my memory, I am still going through fight after fight with Bane. The times we have together just get worse, and we both grow angrier, harder, and colder. And we both seem to adapt a partnering spirit. His name is ruthless.

Ruthless plays into all words that are spoken as well as all actions that flow back and forth between Bane and I. I will repeat myself in saying that money solves no problems and buys no peace. Yes, we are financially strapped with bills and a new baby, but we are still living in a $280,000 home at the ages of twenty-six and twenty-seven. We are set up materially in this world but drowning spiritually.

Satan finds his way into our weakness and triggers and continues to play with us like we are his daily dose of video games. I can tell you that it does not matter where you live. I am in turmoil with the individual I lived with, soaking turmoil in my mind. Wherever I am, whatever I am doing, and whoever I am with is living in my hell on earth with me. Turmoil spreads like a poison-filled snakebite.

Bane and I literally breathe, sleep, walk, and build fires in our own world of hell. Neither of us could lift the other one up or out of the dark spiritual holes we would fall into daily. Sometimes it is as if we would personally dig a deep, dark hole for one another and then ever so lightly push each other into a hurtful place.

When one of us is down, upset, stressed, or depressed, we would make the situation worse for one other. I couldn't handle his issues; he couldn't deal with mine. This is all because we have created this mass confusion and evilness in our relationship. I couldn't fight off my own demons, so how am I supposed to fight his and mine? I couldn't.

At this point, Bane and I are involved with DHR. I turn to one of Bane's family members for help and support. Instead of assistance, it gets worse. This family member decides, out all the ways to facilitate us, starting a case on us would be healing and positive. It is far from that. I feel like this is why it is very important to seek the right help from the right listening ears. I feel like it is also important and good for my soul to find the positive truth in situations. This added pain of DHR could be the step to some change.

We have a counselor coming to the house twice a week to meet with us. It is our daily pick-me-up, like a good stout coffee in the morning. The effect of the sessions last a few hours, and then the strengthening knowledge would slowly fade away deep into our minds. We seem like we need constant counseling. Still nothing helps.

One day after a long, seventy-two-hour battle between Bane and I, I couldn't handle it anymore. I call our counselor and ask for help. I need out. But I always say I need out, and I never would go. If I would actually leave, I would depart for three days maximum and come right back. One of my biggest mistakes is letting myself think that I could fix Bane. Once I realize that day that I could not fix him, I know it would take a higher power, God. Then I believe I opened the line of communication back up between my spirit man and God.

The counselor comes to my house and gives me the name of the place where my son and I could go. She says that someone would even come pick us up. I stand there with a hundred dollars in my pocket that I have saved from a birthday card I got. I look at my son and the house around me, and I fight with myself inside my mind once again. All the thoughts come racing through my head, creating confusion, sadness, and fear. How am I supposed to support my son and me? I already signed my daughter over to her grandparents because I was not capable of caring for her financially. This can't happen again. I will not lose my son.

So then I should stay. Everything will work out this next time. I can just keep my mouth closed and just be everything that Bane wants and desires. I will be extremely submissive. I start to blame every fight we ever had on myself. I begin to question why I asked for help. Then the words are about to exit my mouth. I am going to tell her that I changed my mind, I am okay, and everything will be worked out. I don't need to go with her, and I don't need her help.

All of a sudden, I feel a rush of peace, an undying, deep down knowing, a truth, an overwhelming presence of authority, a strength I have never felt before. It is like I am standing on the middle of the beach, and with all these thoughts, a huge, powerful wave comes crashing on my thoughts and me. The wave clears my mind, and just lovingly with the undying hand of God, I let him know that I will be leaving. I will be going to a women and children's home.

I will tell you when God speaks. No thought or question will be able to infiltrate the voice of the Lord. I go. I pack one bag for my son and another for me. I trust my something more, God, Jesus, the undying feeling of the right way to go. God would send me to a place that was gated in, far from normal society. No vehicle and no family or friends. This is where the Lord would start to mold me to his will. He secludes me at this point in my life, away from everything and everyone so he can spiritually cleanse me. I am not seeking him, so by his power, he would find a way to speak to me. This is the God I trust and love. I believe that everyone has had a moment where he or she would call upon the Lord for help but haven't made seeking him a minutely routine.

Well, this would be the rebuilding of my spiritual man, the start of my walk with our Father. By his grace, he saved me and kept my mind in the palms of his hands. I have nothing to fear. I feel true, honest love, and any sort of evil cannot infiltrate my truth. It's time. It is time to change.

11

Honest Love

The Lord Jesus has brought me to a place that is outside normal city living. I am fenced in and have a curfew, and I am living with other women and children who have fled from domestic violence issues. I am placed in a small room with two bunk bed frames and one small bathroom. I have two adults and a small child plus my son in this room with me. There are also about fourteen other rooms filled with people. Everyone is dealing with her own coffins that are full of her deadly past and what seems like a dark future to them.

I believe and know the Lord placed me in this environment to experience all kinds of different souls, beings, flesh, angels, demons, and spirits. One of the largest, permanent lessons I learned while walking day to day in this two-story, pain-filled building is to never come to any understanding or conclusion by what one sees or hears. We, by human nature, love to use a weapon of judgment upon others strictly by what our windows (eyes) of the body allow us to see. Then we listen with the speaker of our flesh (ears) and come to our own self-standing judgment of how we think things truly are. Let me tell you. The spirit of God, the Holy Spirit, has led me through a truth-filled journey full of loving knowledge and see-through wisdom.

The truth of God is not chaotic. It is pure and straight to the deepest root of our being. His truth goes past our five senses. I walk around talking to Jesus every step I take, asking him to please keep my mind and to please make himself known. I am begging him to speak to me.

"Talk to me!" I would scream in my head.

And if I have a few moments alone in my room, I would cry out to him. I would say, "Please hear me! Please know that I am calling upon you. I need you. I am losing myself, and I am homesick for you! Please, Lord, feel my heart."

I would ask why he isn't talking to me. I would yell at him, telling him, "I don't understand what is happening to me, Lord. I feel like I'm in a constant tornado in my life. And now I am here. I don't want to be here!"

Time after time, I would throw these fits of my misunderstanding to the Lord, with no reply back.

Then one day, I am writing in my journal, and one word—one solid word—comes rushing into my mind and the pit of my stomach like a tidal wave. It imprints on me like a tattoo. The word is "read." I realize at that moment that I had packed the Bible my grandmother had given me for Christmas. It's funny what our soul, spirit man, does for our good and our minds and flesh sometimes don't even notice. My spirit man had made sure that this Bible was packed in my one bag I had taken.

The truth about the Bible is that it is our blueprint, instructions, and way through every and any feeling, placement, and situation. The Bible is the outlined directions through life on earth. It is, in fact, our cell phone to God. Well, God is telling me to *read* my manual, to essentially pick up the phone and listen to what he had to say. I pick up my phone (the Bible), and I open it randomly. The Lord has brought me to the crucifixion of Jesus. I read it and put down my Bible. I don't feel anything. I am expecting an immediate release moment. But no. There is nothing.

I keep on through my days, and I come back to the Bible. This time I am downstairs in the common area so it is a Bible from the bookshelf. I open it randomly. I land once again on the crucifixion. I am in shock. I feel something inside my soul spin for joy, excitement, and happiness. I land twice in a row on the crucifixion. This is God talking to me. He is answering me back. The thing is: I know all about Jesus being nailed to the cross. I read it again. What is God wanting me to know? Hear? Be at peace with? I meditate, pray, and have a microscope on what I had read.

That night I couldn't sleep. I feel energized and awakened in my spirit. I experience the push to walk outside in the back common area of where I am staying. The time is about two thirty in the morning so no one else is awake. I walk outside and look up at the stars, and immediately my body falls to its knees.

I start to pray, "Jesus, I love you so much …"

Then I feel this rush through my whole body. It feels like a wave of heat storming through me. I close my eyes and start crying uncontrollably. I am on the ground with my head between my arms and my knees to my chest. I am professing my love for Jesus. I start to notice that my true eyes, the eyes of my spirit, are opening. This reality I am walking into is just as solid, if not more real, as the earth we walk on day to day. The Holy Spirit has placed me at the foot of the cross. I am now at this moment, kneeling in front of Jesus Christ. I hear it in my spirit. I feel it in my soul. He lets me know at that moment that he truly loves me.

The honesty here is that no words can explain or define the healing that was happing at that moment inside my soul. Jesus changes everything. I cry and cry. I watch the blood pour out of him and feel the pain he encountered for me, actually for all of us. He was on the cross, telling me that he did this for me and every single one of us. This is what love feels like. He is what love means. He is our knowing and our peace. I repent at the cross that night of all that had weighed on me for years, hours, and minutes. All the guilt, shame, hate, anger, and demons are laid in front of the Lord that night. I lay my body bare for him. I need Jesus to take all the splinters, pain, and torment. I need him to remove the evil out of me, to forgive me of my sins, and to renew me with him—his sprit, his life, and his love. Most of all, I need to know and have a relationship with Jesus.

Jesus forgives everything and everyone. He forgives me

of all my sins. He gives me the greatest peace. Knowing I am forgiven, Jesus fills me with the gift and strength of love that he has. And he asks me to forgive all the people who have brought the implants of pain into my life. I grab on to him. I hold on so tight to the love of forgiveness. My spirit with the strength of Christ moves through and touches all the ones I had blamed for my heartaches, scars, and problems.

I spiritually go through and cry out for them for the Lord to touch them like he has blessed me with his hand. I give them all a spiritual kiss. At that moment, my body feels the effects of what is happening spiritually. I feel like a 210-pound man had gotten up from sitting on my back. Spiritually I see it is a large, winged servant of Satan that has detached from me like a leech in the name of Jesus. The Lord gives me a tool, the key to releasing this demon that accumulated negative weight throughout my life that was holding me down. My tool is to repent of my sins, to release everything bare to the Lord, to feel and place what he did on the cross in my heart.

All my deepest darkest secrets he held with him as he sacrificed his body on the cross. He bled for Me; his blood covered me. He took everything and forgave me. It's the greatest love. He renewed all of me. I am healed that night of all mental torment, every hateful thought toward others and myself. I am brought to life. I truly believe that, once you surrender to the Father, you will have the answer you have been searching for.

I searched and searched. My searching was called sin. Instead of feeling like we have to search for something, we need to realize that we do not need to look around. Jesus is here. He already paid the price for us. And the answer to what we are looking for is to surrender everything we are to him, and he will reveal honest love to us. His glory is touchable through belief that Jesus died for us.

We need to hold on to his hand and keep the tools of Jesus within us. Forgiveness unlocks and releases generational curses, heals your family, and puts pieces that were broken back together. Jesus was my antidote to Satan's venomous ways.

Prayers and Understanding

This next section is words and prayers. They have been spoken to my heart as well as come from my heart while I cry out to Jesus during my day-to-day journey with him.

- Love is the most powerful weapon for victory, healing, mending wounds, and bringing a dead spirit back to life. Don't be afraid to love hard, because once true love is unleashed, no one can strip you of it. Emotional pain cannot infiltrate true love. There is only a supernatural power to change everything to beauty in the midst of the actions of love. I pray we can all find this place. Find it even though this world may be dark. Discover it even when people take advantage of your love. Listen! Even if you can't see the change with your natural eyes, open up your spiritual eyes and know that your power of love is winning. How do you know? You know because love itself already won on the cross.

- There will always be a void that no one else but Jesus can fill. So in your constant endless search for fulfillment, remember this answer, Jesus.
- One moment at a time, breathe in grace. Soak in mercy.
- If it hurts, it is working. Let it take its course. Find the purpose in the pain. When you find yourself healed, help your neighbor.
- Sometimes I can't. But then I remember that he can. We are not broken. He, Jesus, is with us.
- Do not become a weapon. Do not be an armament of affliction onto others. Don't allow yourself to be used by the evil one. Clean your heart. Be rooted in Christ. Be the light. You have gone through the valley of the shadow of death and have feared no evil because of divine protection. Don't repay evil with evil. Take the afflictions of Satan and turn his weapons into light. Help others in Jesus's name. We need to take our experiences, trials, and tribulations we have lived through this life to help pull others out of their darkness.
- I can see the pain in your eyes. I understand all of it. I understand the unbelief of what just happened. You will make it through. It doesn't mean it won't hurt. The process without sedation is a guidance to sober healing. Let healing move through your body, and for a moment, let go and let God!
- Jesus, take it from me. I am holding on so tight. Please take it from my hands. My free will and

spirit want to lay it at the cross, but my flesh is sitting in this world, wanting to take it all on myself. All of this chaos is distracting me from my present moment. I am losing time by thinking about how to handle this when it is not mine to deal with. You are my Father in heaven. I believe you have your hand in this. You have to. You are God.

- It is not easy putting everything that issuing on in your hands. It hurts. This hole in my stomach keeps growing. I need you, please. My faith is strong, but my strength is weak. Please, Jesus, I know you hear me and see me. I need you to please take this and make a move on the situation. Change it. I can't do anything about it but stand firm in you and pray. So I am praying hard that your timing is soon.

- It's not even about you trying to bring me down, antagonize me, or push my weak points. This is my test. I can talk the talk about my powerful God, but can I walk the walk? I stand with Jesus through my trials because, by his grace, my faith in him moves me to talk the talk and walk the walk.

- There is a lot on my mind: faith, heaven, Jesus, and the fact we will all die soon. Our life on this earth is temporary. Look at our history books or watch the History Channel. Those people were once alive. Now they are gone. The way we are choosing to live our lives in this current age is so sad and scary. Some are letting Satan use them as his little puppets. Sorrow fills my heart. I wish I could shake some and say "Wake up!" We don't have time to keep bathing in sin. We don't have these moments to continue not knowing the true meaning of love. All it takes is one sentence, "Jesus, help me. I need you, and I believe in you." After one sentence, purpose fulfills your life. Watch the love heal. I love you. Jesus saves.

- I am praying for your strength in God, Jesus, and the Holy Spirit to be working in you and bring you to the next level of mental, spiritual, and physical strength in God. I adore you. I would do anything for you. I will always have your back. Blow them all away with your maturity and growth. Excel today! Excel higher than ever! Stay in Christ Jesus with love, truth, and understanding. He knows your heart and everything you are thinking and doing. God only wants to help. Remember we all have tests in life, some big and others small. These tests are to see where our spiritual, mental, and physical growth is currently standing. I pray you see the truth and pass them all in Jesus's name. Lean into love (Jesus), and you will succeed.

- She calmed the darkest of them all with a word, a heart full of love, and protection for the depths of their souls, knowing that her main goal is to show safety, understanding, and light for the ones trapped in chains to release the chains and set them free with one word, Jesus.

- I feel like being humble allows us to step away from the demands of this world, the labels, the noise, and the ego of this age. I feel like, when we choose humility, we are opening up the purity of our heart to hear God's voice. The supernatural love that dwells in the choice to be humble is life-changing.

- He spoke to my desperate heart. He said, "Don't take your eyes off me. Stay with me. Stay at my pace." So I hold on tightly through every moment, breathing deeply with his strength.

- Maybe we should stop drowning him out. Jeremiah 33:3 says, "Call to me and I will answer you and tell great and unsearchable things you do not know."

- Selfishly I had my box that I wanted you to fit in. It required you to change who you were—your actions, personal guilt, responsibilities, heart, mind, and soul. I realized argument after argument that I am not your creator. I am not your savior. I was always looking to change you instead of looking at myself. I chose you to be apart of my heart. of my heart, and with that choice comes love, selflessness, patience, prayer, faith, strength, and understanding. You are amazingly beautiful. You are you. Just don't let the world or the attacks of the devil control the beauty of your heart and soul. Your salvation depends on the truth. I can't change you. He (Jesus) can though, if you want it. My box is gone and has been laid at the cross. I love you.

- If we are willing to listen, our elders can and will teach us a lot. If we listen, maybe we will be able to avoid heartaches by taking our own road. If we listen, maybe when we get to the divided path we will remember their wise words of wisdom and choose the strengthened way, the route that provides peace and understanding. If we listen, maybe we would understand the importance of love while walking this life. Understand the importance of avoiding pettiness so we may live the secret to life and love our neighbor. We can be taught so much. But are we listening? Proverbs 22:6 says, "Start children off the way they should go, and even when they are old they will not turn from it."

- Sometimes my heart aches for something, yearning for things deeper then they appear in my current reality. With my own self and my own heart's desires, I present my requests to God with thanksgiving and prayer. I wonder if the things I request are not meant for this world. I wonder if they are waiting for me in the next. Or did my flesh continue to do as it pleased and rerouted my life away from the blessings that were waiting for me? I wanted the now. So I did my timing. I didn't wait on God. But I do now. And I wonder many times if I have already missed the train on my heart's fullness in these requests. Philippians

4:6 says, "Do not be anxious about anything, but in every situation, by prayer and petition, with thanksgiving, present your request to God."

- A light shines so bright that it blinds you with peace. So you follow this light of love with faith. Everything is on the line. This light is even in the darkest corners of the world. Believe.

- When you are selfless, God does some supernatural things in your heart, your spirit, and your world. Believe that.

- Stand firm in victory. Jesus is victory.

- Let this soak in. We are fighting a battle that has already been won. Don't get distracted by Satan. Don't let him have you or your family, attitude, heart, and mind. Don't let him have anything while you are here on this earth. Remember the battle is won. How great is your faith?

- Cry out in truth and watch him work. Let God. We just need to obey. The Bible is the blueprint to life, life in the physical body, and life in the spiritual.

- What is beauty? Well, beauty is fleeting. What does fleeting mean: brief, short-lived, or momentary? Think about that for a minute. A woman who fears the Lord is to be praised. Where are our hearts on our beauty or the Lord? One is short-lived; the other is eternal. Holy Spirit spoke this to my heart while reading Proverbs 31:30.

- I guess the art of the craft of feeling lonely and unworthy comes from a place of love, a site of love from God. So in knowing this, we should see this as a gift. He allows us to feel these emotions so that, in the season of loneliness, we make the choice to believe, to lean into the unseen, the truths, the miracles, Jesus.

• Life throws us curveballs, but God is there to knock them out of the park.

• He has given us a roar. A roar in the form of prayer that will cast out all evil. that will cast out evil, a reverberation you will hear in the spiritual realm and feel it leak down into this world. We all have one, just different sounds.

• The Holy Spirit revealed the reason for waking me up this morning at 4:44. He said, "I need you at the right place at the right time." Amen.

• Don't let the artificial light become your source of seeing in the darkness. Open up the windows of your heart (Holy Spirit) and let the real light (Jesus) in.

• Listen, please. No matter who you are, these bottles or these pills do not define who you are! No person in this world can define you. Don't let them drown you in bottles. You are not crazy. You might be hurting deeply, and these bottles numb the pain. They think and feel for you. Emotions no longer mean anything. They temporarily push away the demons. But when you come down, they come back worse than before. And they keep getting worse because you refuse to face them with the power and authority that God has given us through Jesus. Discern between spirits. Is this medicine for life or death, or is the prescription used just to escape?

- If you see someone running and his or her shoelace is untied, will you stop and tell him or her? Or do you let him or her take a chance of falling? Now catch it. Ask this question daily about how you see yourself react when others are in the possible danger zone. Come on, my brothers and sisters in Christ. Don't pass by people who are in danger of falling. Stop and help them. Take their hand. If they choose not to tie their shoelaces, that's on them.

- When you threaten someone, get angry, yell, cuss, call names, bully, or hurt mentally or physically, you have to remember the person you are abusing in any way is a child of God. So be careful whom you decide to push around because, once you mess with someone's child, the father will protect his own. On the other hand, forgiveness is power. The people who are full of darkness can be saved by the example of light that is within you. Christ died for us, specifically all of us. So I would encourage repentance on one side and forgiveness on the other. And I recommend love for all.

- He is the Great I Am. And I am leaning hard into the cross today, tilting in hard at how Jesus was beaten and mangled because he loves us so much. I am sloping into who he is with tears in my eyes. I don't want to be a slave to my anxiety medication (Xanax). It says in the Bible to cast all your anxieties on him. I want that, not something I take with water.

- Sitting down by the seashore, I see the sun rising on the skyline, thinking about how to take a piece of it and store it in my pocket, along with the raindrops I have been loading up on for another day. That piece of sunshine will stay with me. I will hold it in my hand when walking through the dark. It will form a large orb of light around my body, keeping it physically protected from harm. This piece of the sun, this shining light of protection, will allow me to step outside my body with no fear of destruction to the vessel. I will flow in my spirit being able to see from all angles, not just through the eyes of the vehicle I for so long defined myself as, this large piece of bone, flesh, meat, and blood. I made my identity based on this walking death trap. But with my piece of sun, I will be able to be free—free from my body, chains, and judgment. I will be able to live in a floating peace in the supernatural spiritual realm. What we cannot see through our human eye, the behind-the-scene incidents, will be exposed. I want my sunshine with me forever. He is called Christ Jesus.

- I woke up in sorrow. My heart physically and spiritually hurts. I know you might not understand, but the pain is real. We are executing each other. Why? Why? Why? Please, please listen. Everybody has a wound that needs to be healed or a mistake that needs to be understood and forgiven. We all have the same beating hearts. We were all made under the same love. Why is everyone so numb to honest love? Because you are engaging in the games of the devil. You are allowing him to put you under a spell. Please wake up. Please put your hand over your loved one's heart and feel the blood flowing through his or her body. Feel his or her breath on your skin. You have people you love and want to protect, but so do the ones who are being killed. Protection should come in a different form! We should be disarming the hate in each other, not building it up. Protection should come in the form of understanding and peacemaking. So then we can protect our loved ones with an honest heart, and protect the stranger standing next to us that we know nothing about. But God created that same stranger with the same mercy and love. Protection of one another is not killing. It's loving and disarming the pain that sits in the evil hearts of those who desire to cause pain. It hurts. My heart hurts. I wish we could all understand how much a greater force loves us. You are safe with Jesus, and you are safe with the ones who follow his command. Love your neighbor as you love yourself. We need you, Lord. Mark 12:31 says, "The second is this: 'Love your neighbor as yourself.' There is no commandment greater than these."

- So think about it in a new light. You feel like you are in a dark, hard, demanding, frustrating, stressful situation. That could be anything you are facing right now in this moment or season in your life. But instead of focusing on all that is putting you in pain, focus on the fact that God is allowing you to be right here and right now in this season and situation because he knows you can fight the spiritual warfare! God built you with the tools and answers to conquer everything. You have to trust that it is in you that you are that powerful because Jesus is with you. You can pray your child out of drug addiction! You can respect your husband. You can fix your marriage. You can forgive. You can walk away from the chains of depression from the daily rat race of life. You are a warrior in Jesus's name. And you are where you are because God wants to show himself and his power through you, your faith, and your love. God has placed you in this spot to rescue yourself and all those around you. Believe it. You are part of the army of the Lord. You can turn it around. And you will. #JesusSaves

- It's okay to talk about the pain of the current season you are in, the confusion of it all, and the whys. It's okay to vent, cry, and feel like you are breaking. But please, with love, hear me. The last thing the enemy wants is to see you leave that conversation praising God! So let it all out! But let the enemy know who is in total control, Jesus.

Praise him through all trials. He has you going through some things so he can use you to pull someone else out of the darkness.

- I know this. I know so much about this. It is very painful, and just because we are physically healthy, we are dealing with a mental warfare that some don't understand. And that is okay. But sometimes it feels like prison. Darkness surrounds your entire being. It's a deadly pain, a knife in your heart. It feels like unwanted drugs flowing through your veins. And people will just look and say, "Oh, you are fine. Just smile. Look at how blessed you are. Just think positive thoughts."

- It is a little more complicated than that. Let me make this clear. I thank God deeply with everything I have inside of me, through all the ups and all the downs, along with all the valleys and all the mountaintops. He is God, and he is the creator of all things. And glory be to my Father, who I trust loves me. It doesn't take away the lot that was assigned to me or the attacks of the evil one through mental anguish. Everyone has a different cross to carry while here on our journey and purpose with the Lord. I pray deeply for anyone who has to live in a pain that no one can visibly see. Some are in physical wheelchairs; others are in mental wheelchairs. Continue to pray! Pray! Pray! Love! Love! Love! We will make it in Jesus's name.

- Yelling gets nobody anywhere. When you choose to yell at someone, all the other person hears is the sound of his or her emotional wall stacking up to block you out. The spirit of brutal anger will only bruise the situation or sometimes collapse it all together. Speak with love, power, authority, prayer, and purpose.

- Don't become what you hate. Don't return evil with evil. If you do, in the end when you look in the mirror, you are reflecting the very thing that hurts you the most. You are stronger than that because he (Jesus) is with you.

- We fly free. But it is a choice. Free will can be your ticket to freedom or your own steel lock on your chains. Choose.

- Love is an action. So don't get upset when you say "I love you" and my response toward your empty words is a side smile. Choose who you want to be: empty words or forever countless acts of life-giving love. You can choose to see the surface of their smile, or you can choose to dig deeper and save their life in Jesus's name. We are here to help, heal, pray, and provide for each other. Jesus saves, and we are his hands and feet. We are his children. Don't close your eyes to the harsh-burning realities of suffering.

- The Holy Spirit makes us all family. It creates us as one. We should do all we can do to help each other through the pain and suffering. We are family. Don't turn your back because you are scared of stepping into the unknown to help someone. When pain realizes it's not alone, that discomfort turns into power to help someone else through it.

• There is a love that transcends everything. There is a love that exists, and it covers a multitude of sins. This love can be activated in us. This love is available through the gift of faith in Jesus. Jesus saves. You go back to the bookstore to pick yourself up another self-help book, only because the first two you bought didn't work. We can't change ourselves. If we could, this world would not be in total chaos, including our lives. Families and marriages would not be suffering. We need a supernatural change of healing from someone else who is pure, an entity who can remove our filth. Jesus does this healing, and he has had only one book on the shelves for ages, the Bible. Keep calm and march on in God's army.

The Journal

I find the importance of having a journal is a secret gift. A journal can be a tool, a safe place for our mind, spirit, and hearts to express and process the times we have been through. If you decide to keep the journal or burn it when you are done, that is up to you. I know that there is a place of healing that sits in the art of putting our feelings and emotions onto paper. When you bring your unseen emotions and feeling into reality by writing them down, you are taking them out of a hidden place and releasing them out into the open. You are setting the memories free. Do this. Write and process with Jesus. Jesus will fill you with love, understanding, healing, and peace. Writing down emotions that I couldn't put into words but only on paper did something supernatural for me. I always encourage a journal. So here are a few pages just for you to start. Remember you are loved, understood, healed, and heard. I love you. Jesus loves you.

You are Healed.

YOU ARE A CHILD OF GOD.

You are Forgiven.

Jesus will Fill You with Peace.

You can Overcome.

Turn Pain into Power.

LOVE HEALS.

FORGIVENESS BRINGS STRENGTH.

Truth brings Understanding.

YOU HAVE A GREAT PURPOSE.

JESUS SAVES.

YOU ARE LOVED.

YOU ARE FREE.

YOUR CHAINS ARE BROKEN.

YOUR STRENGTH IS RESTORED.

LOOK TO THE CROSS.

Printed in the United States
By Bookmasters